Linux iptables
Pocket Reference

Gregor N. Purdy

Beijing · Cambridge · Farnham · Köln · Paris · Sebastopol · Taipei · Tokyo

Linux iptables Pocket Reference
by Gregor N. Purdy

Published by O'Reilly Media, Inc., 1005 Gravenstein Highway North,
Sebastopol, CA 95472.

O'Reilly books may be purchased for educational, business, or sales
promotional use. Online editions are also available for most titles
(*safari.oreilly.com*). For more information, contact our corporate/
institutional sales department: (800) 998-9938 or *corporate@oreilly.com*.

Editor:	Andy Oram
Production Editor:	Darren Kelly
Cover Designer:	Emma Colby
Interior Designer:	David Futato

Printing History:

August 2004:	First Edition.

0-596-00569-5
[C]

Contents

This book is dedicated to
the memory of my brother
W. Scott Purdy (1969-1995)

Linux iptables
Pocket Reference

Introduction

The Linux kernel's network packet processing subsystem is called Netfilter, and **iptables** is the command used to configure it. This book covers the **iptables** user-space utilities Version 1.2.7a, which uses the Netfilter framework in the Linux kernel version 2.4 and also covers most of what's in 2.6. Because Netfilter and **iptables** are tightly coupled, I will use "**iptables**" to refer to either or both of them throughout this book.

The **iptables** architecture groups network packet processing rules into tables by function (packet filtering, network address translation, and other packet mangling), each of which have chains (sequences) of processing rules. Rules consist of matches (used to determine which packets the rule will apply to) and targets (that determine what will be done with the matching packets).

iptables operates at OSI Layer 3 (Network). For OSI Layer 2 (Link), there are other technologies such as **ebtables** (Ethernet Bridge Tables). See *http://ebtables.sourceforge.net/* for more information.

An Example Command

Here is a sample **iptables** command:

```
iptables -t nat -A PREROUTING -i eth1 -p tcp --dport 80
  -j DNAT --to-destination 192.168.1.3:8080
```

Table 1 shows what this sample **iptables** command means.

Table 1. Decomposed example iptables command arguments

Component	Description
-t nat	Operate on the nat table...
-A PREROUTING	... by appending the following rule to its PREROUTING chain.
-i eth1	Match packets coming in on the eth1 network interface...
-p tcp	... that use the tcp (TCP/IP) protocol
--dport 80	... and are intended for local port 80.
-j DNAT	Jump to the DNAT target...
--to-destination 192.168.1.3:8080	... and change the destination address to 192.168.1.3 and destination port to 8080.

Concepts

iptables defines five "hook points" in the kernel's packet processing pathways: PREROUTING, INPUT, FORWARD, POSTROUTING and OUTPUT. Built-in chains are attached to these hook points; you can add a sequence of rules for each hook point. Each rule represents an opportunity to affect or monitor packet flow.

TIP

It is common to refer to "the PREROUTING chain of the nat table," which implies that chains belong to tables. However chains and tables are only partially correlated, and neither really "belongs" to the other. *Chains* represent hook points in the packet flow, and *tables* represent the types of processing that can occur. Figures 1 through 3 show all the legal combinations, and the order in which they are encountered by packets flowing through the system.

Figure 1 shows how packets traverse the system for network address translation. These are the chains for the nat table.

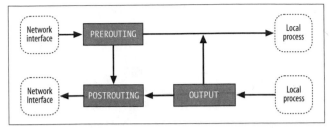

Figure 1. Network packet flow and hook points for NAT

Figure 2 shows how packets traverse the system for packet filtering. These are the chains for the filter table.

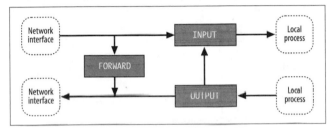

Figure 2. Network packet flow and hook points for filtering

Figure 3 shows how packets traverse the system for packet mangling. These are the chains for the mangle table.

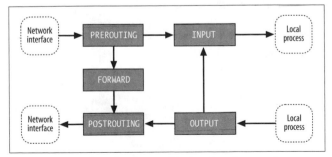

Figure 3. Network packet flow and hook points for mangling

Table 2 shows the five hook points and describes the points in the packet flow where you can specify processing.

Table 2. Hook points

Hook	Allows you to process packets...
FORWARD	... that flow through a gateway computer, coming in one interface and going right back out another.
INPUT	... just before they are delivered to a local process.
OUTPUT	... just after they are generated by a local process.
POSTROUTING	... just before they leave a network interface.
PREROUTING	... just as they arrive from a network interface (after dropping any packets resulting from the interface being in promiscuous mode and after checksum validation).

TIP

For the curious, the hook points are defined in the kernel header file */usr/include/linux/netfilter_ipv4.h* with names like NF_IP_FORWARD, NF_IP_LOCAL_{IN,OUT}, and NF_IP_{PRE,POST}_ROUTING.

Your choice of chain will be based on where in the packet lifecycle you need to apply your rules. For example, if you want to filter outgoing packets, it is best to do so in the OUTPUT chain because the POSTROUTING chain is not associated with the filter table.

Tables

iptables comes with three built-in tables: filter, mangle, and nat. Each is preconfigured with chains corresponding to one or more of the hook points described in Table 2 and shown in Figures 1 through 3. The three built-in tables are described in Table 3.

Table 3. Built-in tables

Table	Description
nat	Used with connection tracking to redirect connections for network address translation; typically based on source or destination addresses. Its built-in chains are: OUTPUT, POSTROUTING, and PREROUTING.
filter	Used to set policies for the type of traffic allowed into, through, and out of the computer. Unless you refer to a different table explicitly, **iptables** operate on chains within this table by default. Its built-in chains are: FORWARD, INPUT, and OUTPUT.
mangle	Used for specialized packet alteration, such as stripping off IP options (as with the IPV4OPTSSTRIP target extension). Its built-in chains are: FORWARD, INPUT, OUTPUT, POSTROUTING, and PREROUTING.

iptables arranges for the appropriate chains in these tables to be traversed by network packets based on the source and destination, and in the order depicted in Figures 1 through 3 and detailed in Tables 4 through 7.

TIP

The default table is the filter table; if you do not specify an explicit table in an **iptables** command, filter is assumed.

Chains

By default, each table has chains, which are initially empty, for some or all of the hook points. See Table 2 for a list of hook points and Table 3 for a list of built-in chains for each table.

In addition, you can create your own custom chains to organize your rules.

A chain's *policy* determines the fate of packets that reach the end of the chain without otherwise being sent to a specific target. Only the built-in targets (see Table 8) ACCEPT and DROP can be used as the policy for a built-in chain, and the default is ACCEPT. All user-defined chains have an implicit policy of RETURN that cannot be changed.

If you want a more complicated policy for a built-in chain or a policy other than RETURN for a user-defined chain, you can add a rule to the end of the chain that matches all packets, with any target you like. You can set the chain's policy to DROP in case you make a mistake in your catch-all rule or wish to filter out traffic while you make modifications to your catch-all rule (by deleting it and re-adding it with changes).

Packet flow

Packets traverse chains, and are presented to the chains' rules one at a time in order. If the packet does not match the rule's criteria, the packet moves to the next rule in the chain. If a packet reaches the last rule in a chain and still does not match, the chain's policy (essentially the chain's default target; see the previous section "Chains" section for more information) is applied to it.

Based on the flow depicted in Figures 1 through 3, the order in which packets are presented to the built-in tables and chains is shown in Tables 4 through 7.

Table 4. Packet flows from one network interface to another (forwarding)

Table	Chain
mangle	PREROUTING
nat	PREROUTING
mangle	FORWARD
filter	FORWARD
mangle	POSTROUTING
nat	POSTROUTING

Table 5. Packet flows from a network interface to a local process (input)

Table	Chain
mangle	PREROUTING

Table 5. Packet flows from a network interface to a local process (input) (continued)

Table	Chain
nat	PREROUTING
mangle	INPUT
filter	INPUT

Table 6. Packet flows from a local process to a network interface (output)

Table	Chain
mangle	OUTPUT
nat	OUTPUT
filter	OUTPUT
mangle	POSTROUTING
nat	POSTROUTING

Table 7. Packet flows from a local process to another local process (local)

Table	Chain
mangle	OUTPUT
nat	OUTPUT
filter	OUTPUT
filter	INPUT
mangle	INPUT

Rules

An **iptables** rule consists of one or more match criteria that determine which network packets it affects (all match options must be satisfied for the rule to match a packet) and a target specification that determines how the network packets will be affected.

The system maintains packet and byte counters for every rule. Every time a packet reaches a rule and matches the rule's criteria, the packet counter is incremented, and the byte counter is increased by the size of the matching packet.

Both the match and the target portion of the rule are optional. If there are no match criteria, all packets are considered to match. If there is no target specification, nothing is done to the packets (processing proceeds as if the rule did not exist—except that the packet and byte counters are updated). You can add such a null rule to the FORWARD chain of the filter table with the command:

```
iptables -t filter -A FORWARD
```

Matches

There are a variety of matches available for use with **iptables**, although some are available only for kernels with certain features enabled. Generic Internet Protocol (IP) matches (such as protocol, source, or destination address) are applicable to any IP packet (described in the reference section "ip (Internet Protocol IPv4) matches," even though the IP matches are available without referencing any match extension).

In addition to the generic matches, **iptables** includes many specialized matches available through dynamically loaded extensions (use the **iptables** -m or --match option to inform **iptables** you want to use one of these extensions).

There is one match extension for dealing with a networking layer below the IP layer. The mac match extension matches based on Ethernet media access controller (MAC) addresses.

Targets

Targets are used to specify the action to take when a rule matches a packet and also to specify chain policies. Four targets are built into **iptables**, and extension modules provide others. Table 8 describes the built-in targets.

Table 8. Built-in targets

Target	Description
ACCEPT	Let the packet through to the next stage of processing. Stop traversing the current chain, and start at the next stage shown in Figures 1 through 3 (and Tables 4 through 7).
DROP	Discontinue processing the packet completely. Do not check it against any other rules, chains, or tables. If you want to provide some feedback to the sender, use the REJECT target extension.
QUEUE	Send the packet to userspace (i.e. code not in the kernel). See the *libipq* manpage for more information.
RETURN	From a rule in a user-defined chain, discontinue processing this chain, and resume traversing the calling chain at the rule following the one that had this chain as its target. From a rule in a built-in chain, discontinue processing the packet and apply the chain's policy to it. See the previous section "Chains" for more information about chain policies.

Applications

The following list provides a brief overview of packet processing techniques and some of their applications:

Packet filtering

Packet filtering is the most basic type of network packet processing. Packet filtering involves examining packets at various points as they move through the kernel's networking code and making decisions about how the packets should be handled (accepted into the next stage of processing, dropped completely without a reply, rejected with a reply, and so on).

Accounting

Accounting involves using byte and/or packet counters associated with packet matching criteria to monitor network traffic volumes.

Connection tracking

Connection tracking provides additional information that can match related packets in ways that are otherwise impossible. For example, FTP (file transfer protocol) sessions can involve two separate connections: one for control and one for data transfer. Connection tracking for FTP monitors the control connection and uses knowledge of the FTP protocol to extract enough information from the control interactions to identify the data connections when they are created. This tracking information is then made available for use by packet processing rules.

Packet mangling

Packet mangling involves making changes to packet header fields (such as network addresses and port numbers) or payloads.

Network address translation (NAT)

Network address translation is a type of packet mangling that involves overwriting the source and/or destination addresses and/or port numbers. Connection tracking information is used to mangle related packets in specific ways. The term "Source NAT" (or just S-NAT or SNAT) refers to NAT involving changes to the source address and/or port, and "Destination NAT" (or just D-NAT or DNAT) refers to NAT involving changes to the destination address and/or port.

Masquerading

Masquerading is a special type of SNAT in which one computer rewrites packets to make them appear to come from itself. The computer's IP address used is determined automatically, and if it changes, old connections are destroyed appropriately. Masquerading is commonly used to share an Internet connection with a dynamic IP address among a network of computers.

Port Forwarding

Port forwarding is a type of DNAT in which one computer (such as a firewall) acts as a proxy for one or more other computers. The firewall accepts packets addressed to itself from the outside network, but rewrites them to appear to be addressed to other computers on the inside network before sending them on to their new destinations. In addition, related reply packets from the inside computers are rewritten to appear to be from the firewall and sent back to the appropriate outside computer.

Port forwarding is commonly used to provide publicly accessible network services (such as web or email servers) by computers other than the firewall, without requiring more than one public IP address. To the outside world, it appears that the services are being provided by the proxy machine, and to the actual server, it appears that all requests are coming from the proxy machine.

Load balancing

Load balancing involves distributing connections across a group of servers so that higher total throughput can be achieved. One way to implement simple load balancing is to set up port forwarding so that the destination address is selected in a round-robin fashion from a list of possible destinations.

Configuring iptables

The procedures for configuring **iptables** vary by distribution. This section provides both generic and Red Hat–specific information on **iptables** configuration.

Persistent rules

On recent Red Hat systems, you can find the **iptables** rules stored in */etc/sysconfig/iptables*. You can determine which runlevels have **iptables** enabled by running the command:

```
chkconfig --list iptables
```

You can enable **iptables** for runlevels 3, 4, and 5 by running the command:

```
chkconfig --levels 345 iptables on
```

You can start **iptables** manually by running:

```
service iptables start
```

You can stop it with:

```
service iptables stop
```

Other configuration files

The kernel's general networking and **iptables** behavior can be monitored and controlled by a number of pseudofiles in the */proc* filesystem. Table 9 lists the most prominent ones.

Table 9. iptables configuration and information files

Path	Purpose
/etc/sysctl.conf	Contains settings for configurations in the */proc/sys* directory that are applied at boot time. For example, */proc/sys/net/ipv4/ip_forward* can be set to 1 at boot time by adding an entry `net.ipv4.ip_forward = 1` to this file.
/proc/net/ip_conntrack	Dumps the contents of the connection tracking structures if you read it.
/proc/sys/net/ipv4/ip_conntrack_max	Controls the size of the connection tracking table in the kernel. The default value is calculated based on the amount of RAM in your computer. You may need to increase it if you are getting `"ip_conntrack: table full, dropping packet"` errors in your log files. See also the entry for */etc/sysctl.conf* in this table.
/proc/sys/net/ipv4/ip_forward	You need to set this to 1 for the host to act as a gateway (forwarding packets among the networks connected to its interfaces). See also the entry for */etc/sysctl.conf* in this table.

Compiling your own kernel

On Red Hat machines, you can determine the kernel you are currently running by looking at the output of the uname -r command, which will print a message such as this:

```
2.4.20-20.9
```

Using your kernel version and your machine type, which can be determined by consulting the output of uname -a (see the manpage for **uname** for more information), you can find the most appropriate configuration file to use to build your new kernel in a file named something like this (we'll use i636 for this example): */usr/src/linux-2.4.20-20.9/configs/kernel-2.4. 20-i686.config.*

The **iptables** configuration settings are found in entries with names like CONFIG_IP_NF_*.

The following configuration options must be selected, at a minimum:

- CONFIG_PACKET (direct communication with network interfaces)
- CONFIG_NETFILTER (the basic kernel support required by **iptables**)
- CONFIG_IP_NF_CONNTRACK (required for NAT and masquerading)
- CONFIG_IP_NF_FILTER (adds the filter table)
- CONFIG_IP_NF_IPTABLES (the basic support for user space **iptables** utility)
- CONFIG_IP_NF_MANGLE (adds the mangle table)
- CONFIG_IP_NF_NAT (adds the nat table)

WARNING

You might be tempted to turn on CONFIG_NET_FASTROUTE, since fast routing sounds pretty attractive for a firewall computer. Don't do that; fast routing bypasses Netfilter's hooks.

The following configuration options provide compatibility layers with older firewalling technologies:

- CONFIG_IP_NF_COMPAT_IPCHAINS
- CONFIG_IP_NF_COMPAT_IPFWADM

Connection Tracking

iptables associates packets with the logical connections they belong to (it even considers certain UDP communication patterns to imply connections even though UDP is a connectionless protocol). In order to do this, it tracks the progress of connections through their lifecycle, and this tracking information is made available through the conntrack match extension.

Although the underlying TCP connection state model is more complicated, the connection tracking logic assigns one of the states in Table 10 to each connection at any point in time.

Table 10. Connection tracking states

State	Description
ESTABLISHED	The connection has already seen packets going in both directions. See also SEEN_REPLY status.
INVALID	The packet doesn't belong to any tracked connections.
NEW	The packet is starting a new connection or is part of a connection that hasn't yet seen packets in both directions.

Table 10. Connection tracking states (continued)

State	Description
RELATED	The packet is starting a new connection, but the new connection is related to an existing connection (such as the data connection for an FTP transfer).

The connection tracking logic maintains three bits of status information associated with each connection. Table 11 contains a list of these status codes as they are named in the conntrack match extension (the --ctstatus option).

Table 11. Connection tracking statuses

Status	Description
ASSURED	For TCP connections, indicates the TCP connection setup has been completed. For UDP connections, indicates it looks like a UDP stream to the kernel.
EXPECTED	Indicates the connection was expected.
SEEN_REPLY	Indicates that packets have gone in both directions. See also ESTABLISHED state.

The **iptables** connection tracking logic allows plug-in modules to help identify new connections that are related to existing connections. You need to use these plug-ins if you want to make multiconnection protocols work right across your gateway/firewall. Table 12 shows the main connection tracking "helper" modules.

To use these, you need to run the **modprobe** command to install the kernel module. See also the helper match extension.

Table 12. Connection tracking helper modules

Helper	Protocol
ip_conntrack_amanda	Amanda backup protocol (requires CONFIG_IP_NF_AMANDA kernel config)
ip_conntrack_ftp	File Transfer Protocol (requires CONFIG_IP_NF_FTP kernel config)

Table 12. Connection tracking helper modules (continued)

Helper	Protocol
ip_conntrack_irc	Internet Relay Chat (requires `CONFIG_IP_NF_IRC` kernel config)
ip_conntrack_tftp	Trivial File Transfer Protocol (requires `CONFIG_IP_NF_ TFTP` kenel config)

Accounting

The kernel automatically tracks packet and byte counts for each rule. This information can be used to do accounting on network usage.

For example, if you add the following four rules to a machine serving as an Internet gateway (assuming two network interfaces: eth0 for the internal network, and eth1 for the Internet connection), the kernel tracks the number of packets and bytes exchanged with the outside world.

```
iptables -A FORWARD -i eth1
iptables -A FORWARD -o eth1
iptables -A INPUT -i eth1
iptables -A OUTPUT -o eth1
```

After running these commands, iptables -L -v shows (note the counts for INPUT and OUTPUT; the nonzero counts indicate that some traffic had already traversed the chains by the time we displayed the counts):

```
Chain INPUT (policy ACCEPT 27 packets, 1728 bytes)
 pkts bytes target prot opt in   out source    destination
    3   192        all  --  eth1 any anywhere  anywhere

Chain FORWARD (policy ACCEPT 0 packets, 0 bytes)
 pkts bytes target prot opt in   out  source    destination
    0     0        all  --  eth1 any  anywhere anywhere
    0     0        all  --  any  eth1 anywhere anywhere

Chain OUTPUT (policy ACCEPT 21 packets, 2744 bytes)
 pkts bytes target prot opt in   out  source   destination
    3   192        all  --  any  eth1 anywhere anywhere
```

See the discussion of the -c, -n, -t, and -x options in
Table 14, and the -L and -Z options in Table 15 to learn
more about the **iptables** options applicable to accounting
applications.

Network Address Translation (NAT)

NAT is the modification of the addresses and/or ports of network packets as they pass through a computer. The computer performing NAT on the packets could be the source or
destination of the packets, or it could be one of the computers on the route between the source and destination.

WARNING

Network address translation requires connection tracking, and connection tracking only works when the computer sees all the packets. So, if your firewall setup
involves more than one computer, take care not to break
connection tracking.

NAT can be used to perform a variety of useful functions
based on the manipulations of addresses and ports. These
functions can be grouped based on which addresses (source
or destination) are being manipulated.

The nat built-in table is intended specifically for use in NAT
applications.

The **iptables** NAT logic allows plug-in modules to help han-
dle packets for protocols that embed addresses within the
data being exchanged. Without the helper module, the packets would be modified to go to different hosts, but the application data being exchanged would still use the pre-NAT
addresses, keeping the application from working.

To use these, you need to run the **modprobe** command to
install the kernel module. Table 13 lists the NAT helper
modules.

Table 13. NAT helper modules

Helper	Protocol
ip_nat_amanda	Amanda backup protocol (requires CONFIG_IP_NF_NAT_AMANDA kernel config)
ip_nat_ftp	File Transfer Protocol (requires CONFIG_IP_NF_NAT_FTP kernel config)
ip_nat_irc	Internet Relay Chat (requires CONFIG_IP_NF_NAT_IRC kernel config)
ip_nat_snmp_basic	Simple Network Management Protocol (requires CONFIG_IP_NF_NAT_SNMP_BASIC kernel config)
ip_nat_tftp	Trivial File Transfer Protocol (requires CONFIG_IP_NF_NAT_TFTP kernel config)

If you want certain packets to bypass NAT, you can write rules that match the packets you are interested in and jump to the special target ACCEPT. You need to have such rules before your other NAT rules.

```
iptables -t nat -i eth1 ... -j ACCEPT
```

Source NAT and Masquerading

Source NAT (SNAT) is used to share a single Internet connection among computers on a network. The computer attached to the Internet acts as a gateway and uses SNAT (along with connection tracking) to rewrite packets for connections between the Internet and the internal network. The source address of outbound packets is replaced with the static IP address of the gateway's Internet connection. When outside computers respond, they will set the destination address to the IP address of the gateway's Internet connection, and the gateway will intercept those packets, change their destination addresses to the correct inside computer, and forward them to the internal network.

Since SNAT entails modifying the source addresses and/or ports of packets just before they leave the kernel, it is performed through the POSTROUTING chain of the nat table.

There are two ways of accomplishing SNAT with **iptables**. The SNAT target extension is intended for situations where the gateway computer has a static IP address, and the MASQUERADE target extension is intended for situations where the gateway computer has a dynamic IP address. The MASQUERADE target extension provides additional logic that deals with the possibility that the network interface could go off line and come back up again with a different address. Additional overhead is involved in this logic, so if you have a static IP address, you should use the SNAT target extension instead.

You can set up SNAT on the eth1 interface by putting a simple rule on the POSTROUTING chain of the nat table:

```
iptables -t nat -A POSTROUTING -o eth1 -j SNAT
```

The corresponding command for masquerading is:

```
iptables -t nat -A POSTROUTING -o eth1 -j MASQUERADE
```

Destination NAT

Destination NAT (DNAT) exposes specific services on an internal network to the outside world without linking the internal computers directly to the Internet. And as long as there is no more than one service to be exposed on any given port, only one Internet connection (public IP address) is required. The gateway computer redirects connections to the specified ports to the designated internal computers and ports and arranges for return traffic to go back to the original address outside the network.

Since DNAT entails modifying the destination addresses and/or ports of packets just before they are either routed to local processes or forwarded to other computers, it is performed through the PREROUTING chain of the nat table.

For example, to forward inbound connections coming in on a gateway's port 80 (HTTP) to an internal web server running on port 8080 of 192.168.1.3, you could use a rule like this:

```
iptables -t nat -A PREROUTING -i eth1 -p tcp --dport 80
   -j DNAT --to-destination 192.168.1.3:8080
```

Transparent Proxying

Transparent proxying is a way to intercept specific outgoing connections and redirect them to a computer that will service them in the place of the original destination computer. This technique allows you to set up proxies for services without having to configure each computer on the internal network. Since all traffic to the outside world goes through the gateway, all connections to the outside world on the given port will be proxied transparently.

If you have an HTTP proxy (such as Squid) configured to run as a transparent proxy on your firewall computer and listen on port 8888, you can add one rule to redirect outbound HTTP traffic to the HTTP proxy:

```
iptables -t nat -A PREROUTING -i eth0 -p tcp --dport 80
    -j REDIRECT --to-port 8888
```

It is more complicated to transparently proxy to a service running on a different host. You can find details on making this work for Squid in Daniel Kiracofe's "Transparent Proxy with Linux and Squid mini-HOWTO," available online at The Linux Documentation Project's web site (*http://www.tldp.org/ HOWTO/TransparentProxy.html*).

Load Distribution and Balancing

You can distribute load across a number of participating hosts using the nth match extension and the DNAT target extension.

Load balancing is a refinement of load distribution that entails using load statistics for the target hosts to advise the choice of target for packets in order to keep the participating hosts close to equally loaded.

Stateless and Stateful Firewalls

A *firewall* is a gateway computer that restricts the flow of network traffic among the networks it connects.

Stateless firewalls use simple rules that do not require connection or other state tracking, such as matches on combinations of source and destination addresses and ports for certain protocols.

Stateful firewalls allow more advanced packet processing that involve tracking connections and other state, such as keeping track of recent activity by host or connection (such as the `iplimit`, `limit`, and recent match extensions).

iptables supports both types of firewall rules (but see the warning in the section "Network address translation").

Tools of the Trade

There are many networking tools that can come in handy while troubleshooting your firewall or other network functionality. Table 14 provides links for a few of the most common ones.

Table 14. Tools of the trade

Tool	Description
ethereal	Network protocol analyzer. *http://www.ethereal.com/*
Nessus	Remote security scanner. *http://www.nessus.org/intro.html*
nmap	Network mapper. *http://www.insecure.org/nmap/*
ntop	Network traffic probe. *http://ntop.ethereal.com/ntop.html*
ping	Send ICMP ECHO_REQUEST to specific hosts.
tcpdump	Packet capture and dumping. *http://www-nrg.ee.lbl.gov/*
traceroute	Print the route packets take to a specific host. *http://www-nrg.ee.lbl.gov/*

iptables Command Reference

Most of the options for the **iptables** command can be grouped into subcommands and rule match criteria. Table 15 describes the other options.

Table 15. iptables miscellaneous options

Option	Description
-c *packets bytes*	When combined with the -A, -I, or -R subcommand, sets the packet counter to *packets* and the byte counter to *bytes* for the new or modified rule.
--exact	Synonym for -x.
-h	Displays information on **iptables** usage. If it appears after -m *match* or -j *target*, then any additional help related to the extension *match* or *target* (respectively) is also displayed.
--help	Synonym for -h.
-j *target* [*options*]	Determines what to do with packets matching this rule. The *target* can be the name of a user-defined chain, one of the built-in targets, or an **iptables** extension (in which case there may be additional *options*).
--jump	Synonym for -j.
--line-numbers	When combined with the -L subcommand, displays numbers for the rules in each chain, so you can refer to the rules by index when inserting rules into (via -I) or deleting rules from (via -D) a chain.
-m *match* [*options*]	Invoke extended *match*, possibly with additional *options*.
--match	Synonym for -m.
-M *cmd*	Used to load an **iptables** module (with new targets or match extensions) when appending, inserting, or replacing rules.
--modprobe=*cmd*	Synonym for -M.
-n	Displays numeric addresses and ports instead of looking up and displaying domain names for the IP addresses and displaying service names for the port numbers. This can be especially useful if your DNS service is slow or down.

Table 15. iptables miscellaneous options (continued)

Option	Description
--numeric	Synonym for -n.
--set-counters	Synonym for -c.
-t table	Performs the specified subcommand on *table*. If this option is not used, the subcommand operates on the filter table by default.
--table	Synonym for -t.
-v	Produces verbose output.
--verbose	Synonym for -v.
-x	Displays exact numbers for packet and byte counters, rather than the default abbreviated format with metric suffixes (K, M, or G).

Getting help

iptables provides some online help. You can get basic information via these commands:

```
iptables -h
iptables -m match -h
iptables -j TARGET -h
man iptables
```

> **WARNING**
>
> Sometimes there are contradictions among these sources of information.

The iptables Subcommands

Each **iptables** command can contain one subcommand, which performs an operation on a particular table (and, in some cases, chain). Table 16 lists the options that are used to specify the subcommand.

WARNING

The manpage for the **iptables** command in the 1.2.7a release shows a -C option in the synopsis section, but the option does not exist

Table 16. iptables subcommand options

Option	Description
-A *chain rule*	Appends *rule* to *chain*.
--append	Synonym for -A.
-D *chain* [*index* | *rule*]	Deletes the rule at position *index* or matching *rule* from *chain*.
--delete	Synonym for -D.
--delete-chain	Synonym for -X.
-E *chain newchain*	Renames *chain* to *newchain*.
-F [*chain*]	Flushes (deletes) all rules from *chain* (or from all chains if no chain is given).
--flush	Synonym for -F.
-I *chain* [*index*] *rule*	Inserts *rule* into *chain*, at the front of the chain, or at position *index*.
--insert	Synonym for -I.
-L [*chain*]	Lists the rules for *chain* (or for all chains if no chain is given).
--list	Synonym for -L.
-N *chain*	Creates a new user-defined *chain*.
--new-chain	Synonym for -N. Commonly abbreviated --new.
-P *chain target*	Sets the default policy of the built-in *chain* to *target*. Applies to built-in chains and targets only.
--policy	Synonym for -P.
-R *chain index rule*	Replaces the rule at position *index* of *chain* with the new *rule*.
--rename-chain	Synonym for -E.
--replace	Synonym for -R.

Table 16. iptables subcommand options (continued)

Option	Description
-V	Displays the version of **iptables**.
--version	Synonym for -V.
-X [*chain*]	Deletes the user-defined *chain* (or all user-defined chains if none is specified).
-Z *chain*	Zeros the packet and byte counters for *chain* (or for all chains if no chain is specified).
--zero	Synonym for -Z.

iptables Matches and Targets

iptables has a small number of built-in matches and targets, and a set of extensions that are loaded if they are referenced. The matches for IP are considered built-in, and the others are considered match extensions (even though the icmp, tcp, and udp match extensions are automatically loaded when the corresponding protocols are referenced with the -p built-in Internet Protocol match option).

This section describes all of the built-in and extension matches and targets included in **iptables** version 1.2.7a.

TIP

Some options can have their senses inverted by inserting an exclamation point surrounded by spaces, immediately before the option. The options that allow this are annotated with [!]. Only the noninverted sense is described in the sections that follow since the inverted sense can be inferred from the description.

Internet Protocol (IPv4) matches

The built-in IP matches are listed in the later section "ip (Internet Protocol IPv4) matches" in order to keep with the encyclopedic format of this section.

ACCEPT target

This built-in target discontinues processing of the current chain and goes to the next table and chain in the standard flow (see Figures 1 through 3 and Tables 4 through 7).

Only this target and the DROP target can be used as the policy for a built-in chain.

ah match

Match extension for the IPSec protocol's Authentication Header (AH) Security Parameters Index (SPI) field. The destination address and the SPI together define the Security Association, or SA for the packet. Used in conjunction with the -p ah (or -p ipv6-auth or -p 51) protocol specification option. Table 17 describes the single option to this match.

TIP

This match is available only if your kernel has been configured with CONFIG_IP_NF_MATCH_AH_ESP enabled.

Table 17. ah match options

Option	Description
--ahspi [!] *min*[:*max*]	Match the value (if only *min* is given) or inclusive range (if both *min* and *max* are given) for the SPI field of the AH.

For example:

```
iptables -A INPUT -p ah -m ah --ahspi 500 -j DROP
```

See the book *IPv6 Essentials*, by Silvia Hagen (O'Reilly) for more information on the IPv6 protocol. See also esp match.

connmark Match

Match based on the packet's connection mark. Table 18 describes the single option to this match.

Table 18. connmark match options

Option	Description
--mark value[/mask]	Match if the packet's connection mark is equal to value after applying mask.

See also the CONNMARK target extension.

CONNMARK target

Set the packet's connection mark. Table 19 describes the options to this target.

Table 19. CONNMARK target options

Option	Description
--set-mark value	Set the packet's connection mark to the integer value.
--save-mark	Save the packet's mark into the connection.
--restore-mark	Restore the packet's mark from the connection.

See also the connmark match extension.

conntrack match

Match based on information maintained by the connection tracking machinery. Table 20 describes the options to this match.

TIP

This match is available only if your kernel has been configured with CONFIG_IP_NF_MATCH_CONNTRACK enabled.

Table 20. conntrack match options

Option	Description
[!] --ctexpire min[:max]	Match the value (if only min is given) or inclusive range (if both min and max are given) for the connection's remaining lifetime (in seconds).

Table 20. conntrack match options (continued)

Option	Description
--ctorigdst [!] addr[/mask]	Match the original destination address (before NAT).
--ctorigsrc [!] addr[/mask]	Match based on the original source address (before NAT).
[!] --ctproto proto	Match the given protocol. The proto argument can be a protocol number or name. See also Table 37.
--ctrepldst [!] addr[/mask]	Match the replacement destination address (after NAT).
--ctreplsrc [!] addr[/mask]	Match the replacement source address (after NAT).
[!] --ctstate states	Match any of the given connection tracking states. The states argument is a comma-separated list of connection tracking states (see Table 10) or SNAT or DNAT.
[!] --ctstatus statuses	Match any of the given connection tracking statuses. The statuses argument is a comma-separated list of connection tracking statuses (see Table 11). The special value NONE may be used to indicate that none of the status bits should be set.

DNAT target

Perform Destination Network Address Translation (DNAT) by modifying the destination addresses and/or ports of packets. If multiple destination addresses are specified, connections are distributed across those addresses. Connection tracking information ensures that packets for each connection go to the same host and port. Table 21 describes the options to this target.

Table 21. DNAT target options

Option	Description
--to-destination a1[-a2][:p1-p2]	a1 and a2 are used to specify a range of destination addresses. p1 and p2 are used to specify a range of ports (for TCP or UDP protocols).

The DNAT target extension is available only on the PREROUTING and OUTPUT chains of the nat table.

For example, to forward packets coming in on interface eth0 for port 80 to an internal web server listening on IP address 192.168.1.80:

```
iptables -t nat -A PREROUTING -i eth0 -p tcp --dport 80
  -j DNAT --to-destination 192.168.1.80
```

WARNING

When doing this kind of DNAT, it is important to separate internal and external DNS so that internal hosts use the inside address of the web server directly.

See also:

- The REDIRECT target extension for simple redirection to ports on the local machine.
- The SNAT target extension for source NAT.
- The nth match extension for an alternative way of implementing load distribution.

DROP target

This built-in target causes the kernel to discontinue processing in the current chain without continuing processing elsewhere and without providing rejection notices to the sender.

Only the DROP target and the ACCEPT target can be used as the policy for a built-in chain.

See also the REJECT target extension, which will send an ICMP reply to the sender.

dscp match

Use this match to identify packets with particular Differentiated Services Codepoint (DSCP) values in their IPv4 headers. The DSCP field is a reinterpretation of the TOS byte of the IPv4 header. Table 22 describes the options to this match.

Table 22. dscp match options

Option	Description
--dscp *value*	Match if the packet's DSCP field equals *value*, which can be specified in decimal or hexadecimal notation (such as 0x0e).
--dscp-class *name*	Match if the packet's DSCP field value corresponds to DSCP class *name*. The names are AF[1-3][1-4], BE, CS[0-7], and EF. See Table 23 for descriptions of the classes, and Table 24 for the corresponding DSCP values.

At most, one of these options may be specified for any rule.

Table 23 provides descriptions of the classes, and Table 24 shows the corresponding DSCP values.

Table 23. Differentiated Services classes

Class	Description
AF	Assured Forwarding. See RFC 2597, "Assured Forwarding PHB Group" (available online at *http://www.rfc-editor.org/rfc/rfc2597.txt*) for more information on the AF class.
BE	Best Effort.
CS	Class Selector.
EF	Expedited Forwarding. See RFC 2598, "An Expedited Forwarding PHB" (available online at *http://www.rfc-editor.org/rfc/rfc2598.txt*) for more information on the EF class.

Table 24. Differentiated Services class names and values

Name	Value
AF11	0x0a
AF12	0x0c

Table 24. Differentiated Services class names and values (continued)

Name	Value
AF13	0x0e
AF21	0x12
AF22	0x14
AF23	0x16
AF31	0x1a
AF32	0x1c
AF33	0x1e
AF41	0x22
AF42	0x24
AF43	0x26
BE	0x00
CS0	0x00
CS1	0x08
CS2	0x10
CS3	0x18
CS4	0x20
CS5	0x28
CS6	0x30
CS7	0x38
EF	0x2e

See also:

- The DSCP target extension.
- RFC 2474 "Definition of the Differentiated Services Field (DS Field) in the IPv4 and IPv6 Headers" (available online at *http://www.rfc-editor.org/rfc/rfc2474.txt*).
- RFC 2475 "An Architecture for Differentiated Service" (available online at *http://www.rfc-editor.org/rfc/rfc2475.txt*).

DSCP target

Set the DSCP values in IPv4 packet headers. The DSCP field is a reinterpretation of the TOS byte of the IPv4 header. Table 25 describes the options to this target.

TIP

This target is available only if your kernel has been configured with `CONFIG_IP_NF_TARGET_DSCP` enabled.

Table 25. DSCP target options

Option	Description
`--set-dscp` *value*	Overwrite the packet's DSCP field with *value*, which can be specified in decimal or hexadecimal notation (such as 0x0e).
`--set-dscp-class` *name*	Set the packet's DSCP field to the value for DSCP class *name*. The names are AF[1-3][1-4], BE, CS[0-7], and EF. See Table 23 for descriptions of the classes, and Table 24 for the corresponding DSCP values.

At most one of these options may be used for any given rule.

For example, to set all outgoing traffic to DSCP 0x0e:

```
iptables -t mangle -A OUTPUT -j DSCP --set-dscp 0x0e
```

See also:

- The dscp match extension.
- RFC 2475 "An Architecture for Differentiated Service" (online at *http://www.rfc-editor.org/rfc/rfc2475.txt*).

ecn match

Match based on values of the Explicit Congestion Notification fields in the IPv4 header. Table 26 describes the options to this match.

Table 26. ecn match options

Option	Description
[!] --ecn-ip-ect [0..3]	Matches the ECN Capable Transport field (two bits) of the IPv4 header.
[!] --ecn-tcp-cwr	Matches the Congestion Window Reduced bit of the IPv4 header.
[!] --ecn-tcp-ece	Matches the ECN Echo bit of the IPv4 header.

See also:

- The ECN target extension.
- RFC 2481 "A Proposal to add Explicit Congestion Notification (ECN) to IP" (available online at *http://www.rfc-editor.org/rfc/rfc2481.txt*).
- RFC 3168 "The Addition of Explicit Congestion Notification (ECN) to IP" (available online at *http://www.rfc-editor.org/rfc/rfc3168.txt*).

ECN target

Set the values of the Explicit Congestion Notification fields in the IPv4 header.

Use this target only in the mangle table. Table 27 describes the options to this target.

Table 27. ECN target options

Option	Description
--ecn-tcp-cwr *n*	Sets the Congestion Window Reduced bit of the IPv4 header to *n* (0-1).
--ecn-tcp-ece *n*	Sets the ECN Echo bit of the IPv4 header to *n* (0-1).
--ecn-tcp-ect *n*	Sets the ECN Capable Transport field (two bits) of the IPv4 header to *n* (0-3).
--ecn-tcp-remove	Clears all the ECN fields of the IPv4 header.

See also:

- The ecn match extension.
- RFC 2481 "A Proposal to add Explicit Congestion Notification (ECN) to IP" (available online at *http://www.rfc-editor.org/rfc/rfc2481.txt*)
- RFC 3168 "The Addition of Explicit Congestion Notification (ECN) to IP" (available online at *http://www.rfc-editor.org/rfc/rfc3168.txt*).

esp match

Match extension for the IPSec protocol's Encapsulating Security Payload (ESP) header Security Parameters Index (SPI) field. The destination address and the SPI together define the SA for the packet. Used in conjunction with the -p esp (or -p ipv6-crypt or -p 50) protocol specification option. Table 28 describes the single option to this match.

TIP

This match is available only if your kernel has been configured with CONFIG_IP_NF_MATCH_AH_ESP enabled.

Table 28. esp match options

Option	Description
--espspi [!] *min*[:*max*]	Match the value (if only *min* is given) or inclusive range (if both *min* and *max* are given) for the SPI field of the ESP.

For example:

```
iptables -A INPUT -p esp -m esp --espspi 500 -j DROP
```

See the book *IPv6 Essentials*, by Silvia Hagen (O'Reilly) for more information on the IPv6 protocol. See also ah match.

FTOS target

This target sets the packet's full Type of Service field to a particular value. It ignores special interpretations of the field such as differentiated services and the various subfields of the Type of Service field. Table 29 describes the single option to this target.

Table 29. FTOS target options

Option	Description
--set-ftos *value*	Set the IP type of service field to the decimal or hex *value* (this target does not accept Type of Service names). See Table 34 for a list of types of service.

For example, this command sets outbound traffic to a normal type of service:

```
iptables -t mangle -A OUTPUT -j FTOS --set-ftos 0
```

See also:

- The tos match extension.
- The TOS target extension for a target that affects just the TOS subfield of the Type of Service field.

helper match

Invoke a connection tracking helper, thereby matching packets for the connections it is tracking. Table 30 describes the single option to this match.

TIP

This match is available only if your kernel has been configured with CONFIG_IP_NF_MATCH_HELPER enabled.

Table 30. helper match options

Option	Description
--helper *name*	Invoke the connection tracking helper *name*. Typical values of *name* are amanda, ftp, irc, or tftp.

For example, to invoke the Internet Relay Chat (IRC) connection tracking helper module to allow related IRC traffic through the firewall, use this command:

```
iptables -A INPUT -m helper --helper irc -j ACCEPT
```

icmp match

Match extension for the Internet Control Message Protocol (ICMP). This match extension is automatically loaded if -p icmp is used. The fields of the ICMP header are shown in Figure 4. Table 31 describes the options to this match.

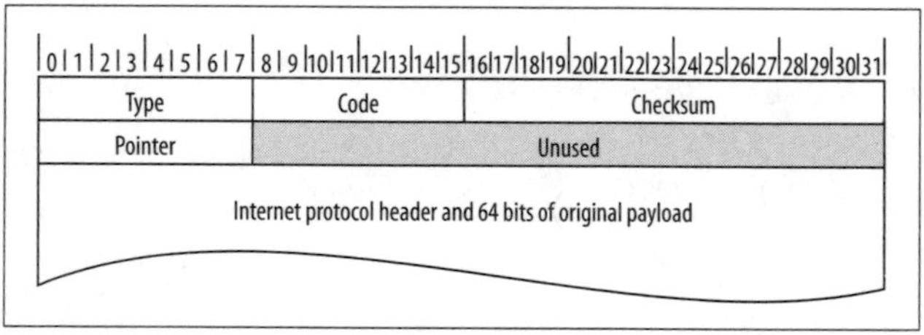

Figure 4. ICMP (RFC 792) header layout

Table 31. icmp match options

Option	Description
--icmp-type [!] *typename*	Matches ICMP type *typename*. See also Table 32.
--icmp-type [!] *type*[/*code*]	Matches ICMP *type* and *code* given. See also Table 32.

Table 32 shows the official ICMP types and codes at the time of writing, from the official database at *http://www.iana.org/ assignments/icmp-parameters* (per RFC 3232, "Assigned

Numbers: RFC 1700 is Replaced by an On-line Database," available online at *http://www.rfc-editor.org/rfc/rfc3232.txt*). The ones in the regular text style (such as type 6, Alternate Host Address) must be referenced by number, not by name.

Table 32. ICMP protocol types and codes

Type	Code	Name
0	any	echo-reply or pong
1	any	*Unassigned*
2	any	*Unassigned*
3	any	destination-unreachable
	0	network-unreachable
	1	host-unreachable
	2	protocol-unreachable
	3	port-unreachable
	4	fragmentation-needed
	5	source-route-failed
	6	network-unknown
	7	host-unknown
	8	Source Host Isolated
	9	network-prohibited
	10	host-prohibited
	11	TOS-network-unreachable
	12	TOS-host-unreachable
	13	communication-prohibited
	14	host-precedence-violation
	15	precedence-cutoff
4	any	source-quench
5	any	redirect
	0	network-redirect
	1	host-redirect
	2	TOS-network-redirect

Table 32. ICMP protocol types and codes (continued)

Type	Code	Name
	3	`TOS-host-redirect`
6	*any*	Alternate Host Address
7	*any*	*Unassigned*
8	*any*	`echo-request` or `ping`
9	*any*	`router-advertisement`
	0	Normal router advertisement
	16	Does not route common traffic
10	*any*	`router-solicitation`
11	*any*	`time-exceeded` or `ttl-exceeded`
	0	`ttl-zero-during-transit`
	1	`ttl-zero-during-reassembly`
12	*any*	`parameter-problem`
	0	`ip-header-bad`
	1	`required-option-missing`
	2	Bad Length
13	*any*	`timestamp-request`
14	*any*	`timestamp-reply`
15	*any*	Information Request
16	*any*	Information Reply
17	*any*	`address-mask-request`
18	*any*	`address-mask-reply`
19-29	*any*	*Reserved*
30	*any*	Traceroute
31	*any*	Datagram Conversion Error
32	*any*	Mobile Host Redirect
33	*any*	IPv6 Where-Are-You
34	*any*	IPv6 I-Am-Here
35	*any*	Mobile Registration Request
36	*any*	Mobile Registration Reply

Table 32. ICMP protocol types and codes (continued)

Type	Code	Name
37	*any*	Domain Name Request
38	*any*	Domain Name Reply
39	*any*	SKIP
40	*any*	Photuris
	0	Bad SPI
	1	Authentication Failed
	2	Decompression Failed
	3	Decryption Failed
	4	Need Authentication
	5	Need Authorization
41-255	*any*	*Reserved*

ip (Internet Protocol IPv4) matches

These built-in matches are available without a preceding -m argument to **iptables**. Figure 5 shows the layout of the fields in an Internet Protocol (IPv4) packet. These fields are the subjects of various match and target extensions (including the set of built-in matches described in this section). Table 36 describes the options to this match.

Figure 6 shows the original layout of the TOS portion of the Type of Service field (a collection of one-bit flags) and two more current interpretations. All three versions are shown here because you may see references to any of these interpretations.

Table 33 gives the meanings of the various values for the (historical) Precedence portion of the Type of Service field. Precedence values are not often used in modern networks because the Explicit Congestion Notification and Differentiated Services features reinterpret the historical Precedence and Type of Service interpretations of these bits.

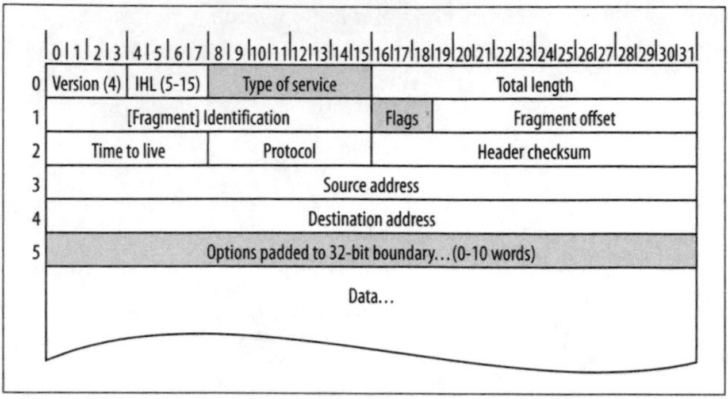

Figure 5. IP version 4 (RFC 791 and RFC 3168) header layout

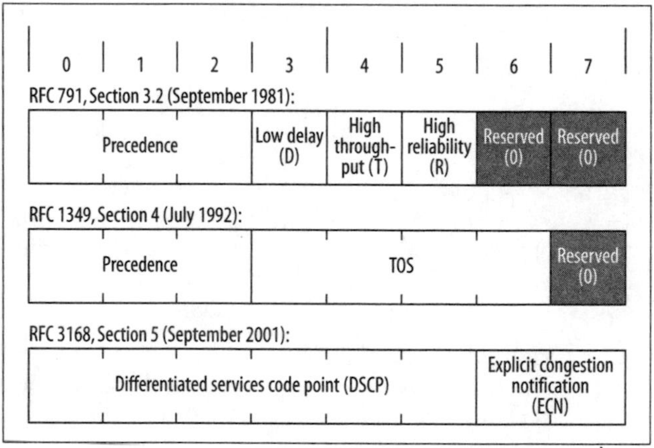

Figure 6. IP version 4 header Type of Service field layout, according to various RFCs

Table 33. IP version 4 precedence values

Code	Description
0	Routine (normal)
1	Priority
2	Immediate

Table 33. IP version 4 precedence values (continued)

Code	Description
3	Flash
4	Flash override
5	CRITIC/ECP (critical)
6	Internetwork control
7	Network control

Table 34 shows the predefined values for the TOS field. Other values are not considered illegal; they just are not defined by the standard.

WARNING

Section 4 of RFC 1349 shows only the values of the four nonreserved bits in the table that correspond to the items in Table 34 here, excluding the implicit zero for the least significant bit. So the binary value 0001 in the RFC corresponds to the full binary value 00010 (decimal "2") in Table 34.

WARNING

RFC 1349 replaces the old (RFC 791 and 1122) bit-field interpretation of the TOS part of the Type of Service IP header field. Of the 32 possible values of the 5-bit field, only the 5 listed above are predefined. Others are still considered legal, but it is no longer permitted to treat the field as a set of one-bit flags.

Table 34. IP version 4 TOS values

Number	Name	Description
0 (0x00)	Normal-Service	Requests normal (default) service.
2 (0x02)	Minimize-Cost	Requests the lowest (monetary) cost path available.

Table 34. IP version 4 TOS values (continued)

Number	Name	Description
4 (0x04)	Maximize-Reliability	Requests the most reliable path available.
8 (0x08)	Maximize-Throughput	Requests the highest throughput path available.
16 (0x10)	Minimize-Delay	Requests the lowest delay path available.

Figure 7 shows the layout of the Flags field.

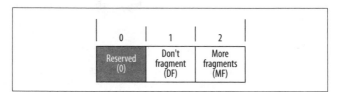

Figure 7. IP version 4 header flags field layout

The complete list of registered Internet Protocol options is available online at *http://www.iana.org/assignments/ip-parameters*. Table 35 contains a list of some of the more common ones.

Table 35. Common Internet Protocol options

Copy	Class	Number	Value	Description
1	0	3	131	Loose Source Routing (LSR) instructs routers to ensure that the packet is processed by a particular series of routers on its way from the source to the destination, although it is permissible for other routers to be visited along the way. The route taken is recorded, as with the Record Route option.
0	2	4	68	Timestamp (TS) instructs routers to record timestamps in the packet when they process the packet.

Table 35. *Common Internet Protocol options (continued)*

Copy	Class	Number	Value	Description
0	0	7	7	Record Route (RR) instructs routers to record their addresses in the packet so the destination host can examine the path the packet took from source to destination.
1	0	9	137	Strict Source Routing (SSR) instructs routers to ensure that the packet is processed by a particular series of routers on its way from the source to the destination without other routers being visited along the way. The route actually taken is recorded, as with the Record Route option.
1	0	20	148	Router alert (RTRALT) is used to advise routers they should apply extra scrutiny to the packet, possibly pulling it out of the fast path. This can be useful when rolling out a new protocol (see RFC 2113, "IP Router Alert Option," available online at *http://www.rfc-editor.org/rfc/rfc2113.txt*).

The copy bit indicates whether the option should be copied into fragment packets if the original packet is fragmented. The class bits are zero (00 in binary) for network control options or two (10 in binary) for debugging options (the other two values, 1 and 3, are not used). The remaining five bits of the eight-bit value are the underlying option number. (People commonly refer to the options by the eight-bit value rather than the underlying five-bit option number.)

Table 36 provides a list of the Internet Protocol match options.

Table 36. *Internet Protocol match options*

Option	Description
-d [!] *addr*[/*mask*]	Destination address *addr* (or range, if *mask* is given).
--destination	Synonym for -d.
--dst	Synonym for -d.

Table 36. Internet Protocol match options (continued)

Option	Description
[!] -f	Second or further fragment of a packet that has undergone fragmentation. Connection tracking does automatic defragmentation, so this option is not often useful. But if you aren't using connection tracking, you can use it.
--fragments	Synonym for -f. Commonly abbreviated (including in the **iptables** manpage) --fragment.
-i [!] *in*	Input interface *in* (if *in* ends with +, any interface having a name that starts with *in* will match).
--in-interface	Synonym for -i.
-o [!] *out*	Input interface *out* (if *out* ends with +, any interface having a name that starts with *out* will match).
--out-interface	Synonym for -o.
-p [!] *proto*	Protocol name or number *proto*. See Table 37 for a list of common protocol names and numbers. Your system's */etc/protocols* file will be consulted to map official names (in a case-insensitive manner) to numbers. The aliases in */etc/protocols* are not available. See also the official protocol list at *http://www.iana.org/assignments/protocol-numbers*. -p *protocol* includes an implicit -m *protocol* when *protocol* is one of icmp, tcp, or udp.
--protocol	Synonym for -p. Commonly abbreviated --proto.
-s [!] *addr*[/*mask*]	Source address *addr* (or range, if *mask* is given).
--source	Synonym for -s.
--src	Synonym for -s.

You can use the old-style dotted-quad notation for masks such as 192.168.1.0/255.255.255.0, or the newer Common Inter-Domain Routing (CIDR) notation such as 192.168.1.0/24 (see RFC 1591, available online at *http://www.rfc-editor.org/rfc/rfc1519.txt*) for the address specifications of -s and -d.

Table 37 provides a list of some common IP protocols.

Table 37. Common IP protocols

Name	Number(s)	Description
ah	51	Synonym for `ipv6-auth`, built into **iptables** (not typically in */etc/protocols*).
ALL	1, 6, 17	Equivalent to not specifying protocol at all.
esp	50	Synonym for `ipv6-crypt`, built into **iptables** (not typically in */etc/protocols*).
icmp	1	Internet Control Message Protocol
igmp	2	Internet Group Management Protocol
ipv6-auth	51	Internet Protocol (version 6) authentication header
ipv6-crypt	50	Internet Protocol (version 6) encryption header
ospf	89	Open Shortest Path First
tcp	6	Transmission Control Protocol
udp	17	User Datagram Protocol

iplimit match

Match when the number of live connections is less than or equal to the specified *count*. Table 38 describes the options to this match.

Table 38. iplimit match options

Option	Description
[!] --iplimit-above *count*	Number of simultaneous connections per network. A "network" for the purposes of this extension is all IP addresses that are the same after masking off the rightmost n bits, where n is determined by the `--iplimit-mask` option.
--iplimit-mask *n*	Sets the number of bits n of IP addresses that will be masked off before grouping them into logical networks. Defaults to 32. This way, all IP addresses are considered to be in the same "network."

For example, you can create rules that will accumulate byte and packet counts when the connection count is low and when it is high:

```
iptables -A INPUT -m iplimit ! --iplimit-above 10
iptables -A INPUT -m iplimit --iplimit-above 1000
```

Or, to allow no more than 10 simultaneous HTTP connections from each class-C–sized network (24 network bits, 8 host bits), use this rule to drop the over-the-limit connection initiation (SYN) packets:

```
iptables -A INPUT -p tcp --syn --dport 80 -m iplimit
    --iplimit-above 10 --iplimit-mask 24 -j REJECT
```

See also the `limit` match extension for rate-based limited matching.

ipv4options match

Match extension for some common IPv4 options. See Figure 5 for the IPv4 header structure. Table 39 describes the options to this match.

Table 39. ipv4options match options

Option	Description
--ssrr	Strict Source and Record Route option is present. See RFC 791.
--lsrr	Loose Source and Record Route option is present. See RFC 791.
--no-srr	No Source and Record Route option is present. See RFC 791.
[!] --rr	Record Route option is present. See RFC 791.
[!] --ts	Time Stamp option is present. See RFC 791.
[!] --ra	Router Alert option is present. See RFC 2113.
[!] --any-opt	At least one option is present.

For example, use this rule to drop all packets with any option present:

```
iptables -A INPUT -m ipv4options --any-opt -j DROP
```

See also the `IPV4OPTSSTRIP` target extension for a way to strip options out of the IP header.

IPV4OPTSSTRIP target

This target strips off all IPv4 options from the packet's header. See Figure 5 for the IPv4 header structure.

Use this target extension only in the `mangle` table.

For example, this rule strips options from all incoming packets:

```
iptables -t mangle -A PREROUTING -j IPV4OPTSSTRIP
```

See also the `ipv4options` match extension for a way to match packets based on options in the IP header.

length match

Match extension for overall packet length. Table 40 describes the single option to this match.

TIP

This match is available only if your kernel has been configured with `CONFIG_IP_NF_MATCH_LENGTH` enabled.

Table 40. length match options

Option	Description
`--length` *min* `--length` *min:* `--length` *:max* `--length` *min:max*	Match the value (if only *min* is given) or inclusive range (if both *min* and *max* are given) for the overall length of the packet. *min* defaults to zero, and *max* defaults to 65535.

For example, to drop long ping packets, use this command:

```
iptables -A INPUT -p icmp --icmp-type ping -m length
  --length 1000 -j DROP
```

limit match

Match until a packet rate limit is exceeded, then stop matching. Table 41 describes the options to this match.

Table 41. limit match options

Option	Description
`--limit [rate[/unit]]`	The number of packets to let through per *unit* of time. Each time a packet is matched, an internal counter of packets to allow in the future is decreased by one. Further, the counter is increased by one *rate* times every *unit* of time, up to the maximum determined by `--limit-burst`. If no argument is given, defaults to 3/hour. If no *unit* is given, defaults to second.
`--limit-burst [count]`	Set the *count* of packets that will be matched in a single "burst." This value is used to initialize an internal allowed-packet counter (so that up to *count* packets can be matched before the first unit of time), and also determines the maximum value of that counter (so that no more than *count* packets will ever be allowed in a single unit of time). If *count* is not given, defaults to 5.

For example, to accept all pings up to 10 per second, use this rule:

```
iptables -A INPUT -p icmp --icmp-type ping -m limit
  --limit 10/s -j ACCEPT
```

or this rule to drop them if the rate exceeds 10 per second:

```
iptables -A INPUT -p icmp --icmp-type ping -m limit
  !--limit 10/s -j DROP
```

You could also use the limit match with the LOG target to implement limited logging.

See also the iplimit/connlimit match extension for connection-count limited matching and the quota match extension for total traffic limits.

LOG target

Log information about packets to the system's logging facility (**syslog**). Table 42 describes the options to this target.

Table 42. LOG target options

Option	Description
`--log-ip-options`	Include the IP options in the log entries.
`--log-level level`	Log with the specified `level` (by number or name). The default level is `warning`. See Table 43 for a list of logging level numbers and names (names are case-insensitive to **iptables**).
`--log-prefix prefix`	Prefix log entries with `prefix`.
`--log-tcp-options`	Include the TCP options in the log entries.
`--log-tcp-sequence`	Include the TCP sequence numbers in the log entries.

The available logging levels (as shown in Table 43) are those defined in the *<linux/kernel.h>* header file (you may have such a header, but if you don't have full kernel source, you may not have these definitions).

Table 43. Logging levels

Level	Name	Description
0	`emerg` or `panic`	Something is incredibly wrong; the system is probably about to crash.
1	`alert`	Immediate attention is required.
2	`crit`	Critical hardware or software failure.
3	`err` or `error`	Usually used for reporting of hardware problems by drivers.
4	`warning` or `warn`	Something isn't right, but the problem is not serious.

Table 43. Logging levels (continued)

Level	Name	Description
5	notice	No problems: indicates an advisory of some sort.
6	info	General information, such as drivers' reports about hardware.
7	debug	Debugging.

TIP

The names panic, error, and warn are deprecated (although **iptables** still maps err to error for display).

You can determine where the log entries go by looking at your *syslog.conf* file, which should have an entry such as kern.=info *path*. If you use the --log-level info option, log entries will go into the log file at *path*.

See also the ULOG target extension, which provides more advanced logging capabilities.

mac match

Match based on the media access controller (MAC) address of the source Ethernet interface. Table 44 describes the single option to this match.

This is actually not an Internet Protocol match because Ethernet is at a lower level in the network architecture, but because many IP networks run over Ethernet, and because the MAC information is available, this match extension is included.

TIP

This match is available only if your kernel has been configured with CONFIG_IP_NF_MATCH_MAC enabled.

Table 44. mac match options

Option	Description
--mac-source [!] *mac*	Match when the Ethernet frame source MAC field matches *mac*. The format is: *XX:XX:XX:XX:XX:XX*, where each *XX* is replaced by two hexadecimal digits.

Use this only with rules on the PREROUTING, FORWARD, or INPUT chains, and only for packets coming from Ethernet devices. For example, this rule allows only a single Ethernet device to communicate over an interface (such as an interface connected to a wireless device):

```
iptables -A PREROUTING -i eth1 -m mac --mac-source
  ! 0d:bc:97:02:18:21 -j DROP
```

mark match

Match packets that have been marked with a particular value. Packet marking can be used in conjunction with the **ip** command from the **iproute2** tool set for advanced routing applications. Table 45 describes the single option to this match.

The Linux kernel allows you to attach an integer mark to a packet and carries the mark along with the packet as it is processed by other parts of the kernel. Note that the mark is not stored in any IP or other header but is a separate piece of metadata maintained by the kernel. Therefore, packet marks are lost once packets leave the computer on which they were set (as happens if the packet was forwarded to another computer).

TIP

This match is available only if your kernel has been configured with CONFIG_IP_NF_MATCH_MARK enabled.

Table 45. mark match options

Option	Description
--mark *value*[/*mask*]	Match if the packet's mark is *value* after being subjected to *mask*.

The *mask* can be used to treat the kernel's mark value as a set of bit fields although the MARK target extension does not have a *mask*, which prevents you from incrementally setting bit fields with **iptables**.

See also the MARK target extension.

MARK target

Set the packet's mark. Packet marking can be used in conjunction with the **ip** command from the **iproute2** tool set for advanced routing applications. Table 46 describes the single option to this target.

TIP

This target is available only if your kernel has been configured with CONFIG_IP_NF_TARGET_MARK enabled.

This target can be used only from the mangle table.

Table 46. MARK target options

Option	Description
--set-mark *value*	Set the packet's mark to *value*.

See also:

- The mark match extension.
- The TOS target extension for a target that can mark packets in a way that *can* be seen by other computers.

MASQUERADE target

Use this target extension to perform SNAT when the interface has a dynamic IP address. Table 47 describes the single option to this target.

The MASQUERADE target extension is for TCP and UDP connections.

Table 47. MASQUERADE target options

Option	Description
--to-ports *p1*[-*p2*]	Change the source ports of the packets to the port (or range of ports) given.

See also the SNAT target extension for a target with similar
functionality for static IP address connections.

multiport match

Match multiple TCP or UPD ports and port ranges simulta-
neously. Table 48 describes the options to this match.

For use only with TCP and UDP protocols (-p tcp or -p udp).

Table 48. multiport match options

Option	Description
--destination-ports *portspec*	Matches if the destination port is one of the port names or numbers listed.
--dports	Synonym for -destination-ports.
--ports *portspec*	Matches if either the source or the destination port is one of the port names or numbers listed.
--source-ports *portspec*	Matches if the source port is one of the port names or numbers listed.
--sports	Synonym for -source-ports.

Port specifications (*portspec*, above) are comma-separated lists of up to 15 individual ports or port ranges (2 ports separated by a colon).

NETLINK target

Send packets to userspace via a netlink socket. You can use this to call your own custom packet processing code in user space or to plug into an external application such as **fwmon** (see *http://www.scaramanga.co.uk/fwmon/*). Table 49 describes the options to this target.

TIP

This match is available only if your kernel has been configured with CONFIG_IP_NF_QUEUE enabled.

Table 49. NETLINK target options

Option	Description
--nldrop	Send the packet and then drop it.
--nlmark *number*	Mark the packet with *number*.
--nlsize *size*	Send only the first *size* bytes of the packet.

For example, to send all ICMP ping traffic to **netlink** and then drop it, use this command:

```
iptables -A INPUT -p icmp --icmp-type ping -j NETLINK
  --nldrop
```

See also:

- The ULOG target extension, which uses **netlink** sockets to communicate with the ulogd userspace packet logging daemon.
- The **netlink** manpages (usually visible by running man 7 netlink or man 3 netlink) for more information.
- RFC 3549 "Linux Netlink as an IP Services Protocol" (online at *http://www.rfc-editor.org/rfc/rfc3549.txt*).

NETMAP target

An IPv4 address consists of 32 bits, divided into a network number and a host number based on the network mask. This target strips off the network number and replaces it with a different network number, effectively mapping the hosts of one network to another. This target alters the destination address in the PREROUTING chain for incoming packets, or the source address in the POSTROUTING chain for outgoing packets. Table 50 describes the single option to this target.

TIP

This match is available only if your kernel has been configured with CONFIG_IP_NF_TARGET_NETMAP enabled.

Table 50. NETMAP target options

Option	Description
--to addr[/mask]	Map hosts to the addr[/mask] network.

For example, to map between the networks 192.168.1.0/24 and 172.17.5.0/24, use these commands:

```
iptables -t nat -A PREROUTING -d 192.168.1.0/24 -j NETMAP
    --to 172.17.5.0/24
iptables -t nat -A POSTROUTING -s 172.17.5.0/24 -j NETMAP
    --to 192.168.1.0/24
```

nth match

Match one out of every group of *n* packets matching earlier rule criteria. Table 51 describes the options to this match.

Table 51. nth match options

Option	Description
--counter num	Use packet counter num for this rule. There are 16 packet counters available, and the default is zero. You can use different packet counters for different packet streams on which you are going to use the nth match extension.

Table 51. nth match options (continued)

Option	Description
--every *n*	Match one out of every group of *n* packets.
--packet *num*	Specify which one (*num*) of each group of *n* packets to match. If you use --packet in any rule, you must use it in *n* different rules, covering the cases from zero to *n* - 1. The default is zero, so that just specifying --every *n* gives you packet zero out of every group of *n*.
--start *num*	Start the counter at *num* instead of the default, which is zero.

For example, to distribute incoming load across three servers:

```
iptables -t nat -A PREROUTING -i eth0 -p udp --dport $PORT
  -m nth --every 3 --packet 0 -j DNAT --to-destination
  $SERVER0
iptables -t nat -A PREROUTING -i eth0 -p udp --dport $PORT
  -m nth --every 3 --packet 1 -j DNAT --to-destination
  $SERVER1
iptables -t nat -A PREROUTING -i eth0 -p udp --dport $PORT
  -m nth --every 3 --packet 2 -j DNAT --to-destination
  $SERVER2
```

You could also use the nth match with the DROP target to simulate packet loss.

See also the DNAT target extension for a better way to accomplish load distribution.

owner match

Match packets based on information about the owning (creating) process. This match extension is available only in OUTPUT chains, since it requires access to information about the local process that created the packet. This match extension is ineffective for ICMP packets, which do not have owners. Table 52 describes the options to this match.

TIP

This match is available only if your kernel has been configured with CONFIG_IP_NF_MATCH_OWNER enabled.

Table 52. owner match options

Option	Description
--cmd-owner cmd	Match if the creating process was command cmd. (Not all kernels support this feature.)
--gid-owner gid	Match if the creating process' effective group id is gid.
--pid-owner pid	Match if the creating process' process id is pid.
--sid-owner sid	Match if the creating process is a member of the session group sid.
--uid-owner uid	Match if the creating process' effective user id is uid.

pkttype match

Match packets having a particular packet type that is classified based on the type of destination address it contains. Table 53 describes the options to this match.

TIP

This match is available only if your kernel has been configured with CONFIG_IP_NF_MATCH_PKTTYPE enabled.

See Figure 5 for the IPv4 header structure.

Table 53. pkttype match options

Option	Description
--pkt-type [!] type	Match packets of the given type, which must match one of the types in Table 54.

Table 54. Packet types

Name	Description
bcast	Synonym for broadcast.
broadcast	The destination address is a network broadcast address (all the host bits are one).
host	Synonym for unicast.
mcast	Synonym for multicast.

Table 54. Packet types (continued)

Name	Description
multicast	The destination address is a multicast address (an address in the range 224.0.0.0 to 239.255.255.255).
unicast	The destination address is a host address.

Multicast addressing is discussed in RFC 1112 and RFC 1122, sections 3.2.1.3 and 3.3.6.

pool match

Matches source or destination IP addresses against those in specific pools of IP addresses, which can be populated dynamically via the POOL target. You manage pools with the **ippool** command and the */etc/ippool.conf* configuration file (a map from pool numbers to names), which must be present for the pool match to be useable. Table 55 describes the options to this match.

Table 55. pool match options

Option	Description
[!] --srcpool *pool*	Match if the source IP address is in *pool*.
[!] --dstpool *pool*	Match if the destination IP address is in *pool*.

The *pool* argument can be either a pool number or a name from */etc/ippool.conf*.

See also the POOL target extension.

POOL target

Adds or removes source or destination IP addresses in specific pools, which can be used to match packets via the pool match. You manage pools with the **ippool** command and the */etc/ippool.conf* configuration file (a map from pool numbers to names), which must be present for the POOL target to be useable. Table 56 describes the options to this target.

Table 56. POOL target options

Option	Description
`--add-dstip` *pool*	Add the packet's destination IP address to *pool*.
`--add-srcip` *pool*	Add the packet's source IP address to *pool*.
`--del-dstip` *pool*	Remove the packet's destination IP address from *pool*.
`--del-srcip` *pool*	Remove the packet's source IP address from *pool*.

The *pool* argument can be either a pool number or a name from */etc/ippool.conf*.

See also the pool match extension.

psd (Port Scan Detector) match

This match extension attempts to detect port scans by monitoring connection attempts across port numbers. It calculates and maintains a port scan value statistic (roughly analogous to the number of connection attempts) based on parameters you can set and match with the options described in Table 57.

Table 57. psd match options

Option	Description
`--psd-delay-threshold` *delay*	The maximum *delay* (in ticks, where a tick is typically 1/100 of a second—defined by the kernel's HZ constant) between consecutive connection attempts for them to be considered part of a scan. As long as new connection attempts come no farther apart than this, they will result in an increase to the port scan value. The default is 300.
`--psd-hi-ports-weight` *weight*	The *weight* to assign to high port numbers (those from 1024 and up; also called unprivileged ports) in calculating the port scan value. Each connection attempt to a high port is counted as this many hits. The default is 1.

Table 57. psd match options (continued)

Option	Description
--psd-lo-ports-weight *weight*	The *weight* to assign to low port numbers (those below 1024; also called privileged ports) in calculating the port scan value. Each connection attempt to a low port is counted as this many hits. The default is 3.
--psd-weight-threshold *weight*	Match when the port scan value is greater than or equal to *weight*. The default is 21.

For example:

```
iptables -A INPUT -m psd -j DROP
```

See also the recent match extension for another way of detecting possibly hostile access.

QUEUE target

This built-in target causes the packet to be queued for processing by a userspace application written with the libipq library. You must use the ip_queue loadable kernel module to use the QUEUE target. The */proc/sys/net/ipv4/ip_queue_maxlen* file contains the maximum queue depth, and you can see the queue status at */proc/net/ip_queue*. If there is no userspace application processing the queue, the QUEUE target is equivalent to DROP.

quota match

Match until a quota is reached. Table 58 describes the single option to this match.

Table 58. quota match options

Option	Description
--quota *amount*	Match until the number of bytes of network traffic reaches the quota *amount*, and then stop matching.

For example, to start dropping packets on port $PORT after $QUOTA bytes have been received, use these two rules:

```
iptables -A INPUT -p tcp --dport $PORT -m quota --quota
  $QUOTA -j ACCEPT
iptables -A INPUT -p tcp --dport $PORT -j DROP
```

The quota match doesn't provide a way to reset the quota or to set the quota as a rate limit rather than as a total size limit. See the limit match for more rate limits.

random match

Match packets randomly, based on a probability. This can be used to simulate a bad link to test the robustness of a system. Table 59 describes the single option to this match.

Table 59. random match options

Option	Description
--average *percent*	Set the percent chance a packet will be matched to *percent* (from 1 to 99). The default *percent* is 50.

For example, use this rule to drop 10 percent of incoming ping requests:

```
iptables -A INPUT -p icmp --icmp-type ping -m random
  --average 10 -j DROP
```

realm match

Matches routing realms as defined and used by the **ip** command. This match is used for advanced routing applications. Table 60 describes the single option to this match.

Table 60. realm match options

Option	Description
--realm [!] *value*[/*mask*]	Specifies the realm *value* to match, along with an optional *mask* of the bits to compare. The default mask is 0xffffffff, which causes an exact match.

recent match

Match all traffic from IP addresses that have seen recent activity of a particular kind, as indicated by the options. Table 61 describes the options to this match.

Table 61. recent match options

Option	Description
--hitcount *hits*	Match only if the hit-count for the packet's source address in the designated recent address list is at least *hits*. Used with --rcheck or --update.
--name *name*	Designate the recent address list named *name* to be used for matching or modification. Default is DEFAULT.
[!] --rcheck	Match if the packet's source address is in the designated recent address list.
--rdest	Save the destination address of the packet during --set.
[!] --remove	Match if the packet's source address is in the designated recent address list and remove the packet's source address from the designated recent address list.
--rsource	Save the source address of the packet during --set. This is the default behavior.
--rttl	Match only if both the source address and the TTL of the original --set packet and the current packet match. This stronger matching makes it harder for someone to send packets that look like they are coming from somewhere else, which might cause you to lock out that third party. Used with --rcheck or --update.
--seconds *secs*	Match only if the last-seen timestamp for the packet's source address in the designated recent address list is within the last *secs* seconds. Used with --rcheck or --update.
[!] --set	Add the source address of the packet to the designated recent address list.
[!] --update	Match if the packet's source address is in the designated recent address list and update the last-seen timestamp for the packet's source address in the designated recent address list.

For example, to create a "bad guy" list of addresses connecting to port 139 (imap) and then drop any incoming packets from those addresses, you can use these rules:

```
iptables -A PREROUTING -p tcp --dport imap -m recent --name
  BADGUY --set
iptables -A PREROUTING -m recent --name BADGUY --seconds
  60 -j DROP
```

See also the psd match extension for another way of detecting possibly hostile access. You could use the psd match extension along with the --set option of this match extension to set up an address list based on port scan detection.

record-rpc match

Matches packets with source IP addresses that have previously inquired about the destination port via the RPC portmapper service. This can be useful in filtering out bogus RPC traffic. There are no options for this target.

WARNING

You shouldn't be accepting any RPC traffic over the Internet. If you do, you could be exposing NFS or some other RPC-based service to the world at large. These services are meant more for interactions among mutually trusting hosts, and you shouldn't be extending any trust to hosts at large on the Internet.

See also the configuration file */etc/rpc* for your system's portmapper configuration.

REDIRECT target

Redirects the packet to the local machine by setting its destination IP address to one of the IP addresses of the local machine. If the packet originated locally, its destination address is changed to 127.0.0.1 (the address of the local loopback interface). If the packet came in on a network interface, the first-bound IP address of that interface is used. Table 62 describes the single option to this target.

TIP

This target is available only if your kernel has been configured with CONFIG_IP_NF_TARGET_REDIRECT enabled.

This target is for use with the PREROUTING and OUTPUT chains of the nat table.

Table 62. REDIRECT target options

Option	Description
--to-ports *p1*[-*p2*]	Also modify the destination port, setting it to a value between *p1* and *p2* (inclusive), or just *p1* if *p2* is not specified. By default, the destination port is not altered.

See also the DNAT target extension for more sophisticated destination address manipulation.

REJECT target

Rejects a packet and sends an explicit notification back to the packet's sender via ICMP. While using DROP is usually appropriate for packets originating outside your network, you may want to use REJECT for packets originating inside your network in order to aid in network troubleshooting. Table 63 describes the single option to this target.

TIP

This target is available only if your kernel has been configured with CONFIG_IP_NF_TARGET_REJECT enabled.

This target is available for the INPUT, FORWARD, and OUTPUT chains.

Table 63. REJECT target options

Option	Description
--reject-with *type*	Send a *type* ICMP or TCP rejection reply and drop the packet. See Table 64 for a list of rejection types.

If no --reject-with option is specified, the default *type* is icmp-port-unreachable.

Table 64. REJECT rejection types

Type	Description
host-prohib	Synonym for icmp-host-prohibited.
host-unreach	Synonym for icmp-host-unreachable.
icmp-host-prohibited	Send an ICMP host prohibited reply.
icmp-host-unreachable	Send an ICMP host unreachable reply.
icmp-net-prohibited	Send an ICMP network prohibited reply.
icmp-net-unreachable	Send an ICMP network unreachable reply.
icmp-port-unreachable	Send an ICMP port unreachable reply.
icmp-proto-unreachable	Send an ICMP protocol unreachable reply.
net-prohib	Synonym for icmp-net-prohibited.
net-unreach	Synonym for icmp-net-unreachable.
port-unreach	Synonym for icmp-port-unreachable.
proto-unreach	Synonym for icmp-proto-unreachable.
tcp-reset	Send a TCP reset (with the RST flag set) reply. For use in response to TCP packets only.

See also the DROP target, which doesn't send a reply.

RETURN target

This built-in target is similar to the ACCEPT built-in target, but it is meant for user-defined chains; it returns control to the calling chain (the one that used -j to jump to the current chain).

See also the ACCEPT built-in target.

ROUTE target

Route packets explicitly rather than letting the normal kernel routing logic determine the route, without modifying the packets. This target extension is used only in the PREROUTING chain of the mangle table. Table 65 describes the options to this target.

Table 65. ROUTE target options

Option	Description
--iface *name*	Send the packet from the interface *name*.
--ifindex *index*	Send the packet from the interface with number *index* (based on the order in */proc/net/dev*).

For example, to send matched packets from the eth2 interface:

```
iptables -t mangle -A PREROUTING ... -j ROUTE --iface eth2
```

SAME target

Works like the SNAT target extension, but when using more than one source address, attempts to use the same source address for all connections that request the same destination address. Table 66 describes the options to this target.

Table 66. SAME target options

Option	Description
--nodst	Don't use the destination IP address in selecting the source IP to use for the first connection for a particular destination IP.
--to *a1-a2*	Specify the source address(es) to use. This option can be used more than once to specify multiple ranges.

See also the SNAT target extension.

SNAT target

Use this target extension to perform SNAT when the interface has a static IP address. Table 67 describes the single option to this target.

Table 67. SNAT target options

Option	Description
--to-source *a1*[*-a2*][:*p1-p2*]	Change the source IP address field of the packet to the addresses given (and optionally for the UDP and TCP protocols, ports). This option can be used more than once to specify multiple ranges.

Typical usage involves a single address, although if your host has multiple addresses assigned to its interface, you can use an address range and the SNAT target will distribute the connections across the addresses in the range. You can also specify a range of port numbers if you want to limit the ports that will be used for SNAT. Unless directed otherwise, **iptables** uses unused ports in the range 1–511 if the pre-NAT port is 1–511, unused ports in the range 600–1023 if the pre-NAT port is 512–1023, or unused ports in the range 1024–65535 if the pre-NAT port is 1024–65535.

For example, if eth0 was your network interface connected to the Internet, and the environment variable $STATIC contained the static IP address of eth0 (assigned by your Internet service provider), you could use a rule like this to have your computer apply SNAT to outbound traffic to make it all look as if it is coming from the gateway computer:

```
iptables -t nat -A POSTROUTING -o eth0 -j SNAT
   --to $STATIC
```

See also:

- The DNAT target extension for destination NAT.
- The SAME target extension.
- The MASQUERADE target extension for a heavier-weight target with similar functionality for dynamic IP address connections (which can cause strange failures with the SNAT match extension).

state match

Use connection tracking information to match packets belonging to connections in a particular set of states. Table 68 describes the single option to this match.

TIP

This match is available only if your kernel has been configured with CONFIG_IP_NF_MATCH_STATE enabled.

Table 68. state match options

Option	Description
--state state[,state...]	Match if the connection the packet belongs to is in one of the listed *states*. State must be one of the standard state names (see Table 10)

For example, if your machine is a gateway connected to the Internet on its eth0 interface, you could use this command to prevent it from forwarding packets for connections initiated from the outside:

```
iptables -A FORWARD -m state NEW -i eth0 -j DROP
```

string match

Matches packets containing a particular string anywhere in their payload. This match performs a simple, per-packet string match, so it should not be used by itself to identify traffic to be dropped. This match is intended to be used with the QUEUE target extension to identify packets that should be further examined in user space. Table 69 describes the single option to this match.

Table 69. string match options

Option	Description
--string [!] string	Match packets containing *string*.

For example, to queue any packet containing the string .pif to user space for later examination by an intrusion detection system:

```
iptables -A INPUT -m string --string .pif -j QUEUE
```

The string match won't catch matches across packet boundaries, so the example just shown would fail to match a pair of packets where the first one ended with .p and the next one started with if.

tcp match

Match extension for TCP. This match extension is automatically loaded if -p tcp is used. Table 70 describes the options to this match, and Table 71 provides the TCP protocol flags.

Figure 8 shows the structure of the TCP header.

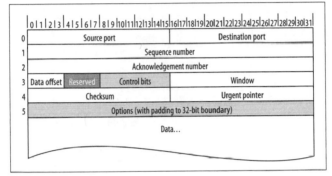

Figure 8. TCP (RFC 793 and RFC 3168) header layout

Figure 9 shows the structure of the Control Bits field of the TCP header.

Congestion window reduced (CWR)	ECN echo (ECE)	Urgent (URG)	Acknow-ledgement (ACK)	Push function (PSH)	Reset connection (RST)	Synchronize sequence numbers (SYN)	No more data from sender (FIN)

Figure 9. TCP header Control Bits field layout

Table 70. tcp match options

Option	Description
--destination-port	Synonym for --dport.

Table 70. tcp match options (continued)

Option	Description
`--dport [!] port[:port]`	Match when the TCP destination port number is equal to *port* (if only one *port* is given) or in the inclusive range (if both *ports* are given). Ports can be specified by name (from your system's */etc/services* file) or number. See Table 74 for high-level port ranges and Table 75 for a list of common ports.
`--mss value[:value]`	Match SYN and ACK packets (see Table 73) when the value of the TCP protocol Maximum Segment Size (MSS) field is equal to *value* (if only one *value* is given) or in the inclusive range (if both *value*s are given). See also the tcpmss match extension.
`--source-port`	Synonym for `--sport`.
`--sport [!] port[:port]`	Match when the TCP source port is equal to *port* (if only one *port* is given) or in the inclusive range (if both *ports* are given). Ports can be specified by name (from your system's */etc/services* file) or number. See Table 75 for high-level port ranges and Table 76 for a list of common ports.
`[!] --syn`	Synonym for `--tcp-flags SYN,RST,ACK SYN`. Packets matching this are called "SYN" packets (see also Table 73). This option can be used to construct rules to block incoming connections while permitting outgoing connections.
`--tcp-flags [!] mask comp`	Check the *mask* flags, and match if only the *comp* flags are set. The *mask* and *comp* arguments are comma-separated lists of flag names from Table 71, or one of the two special values ALL and NONE.
`--tcp-option [!] num`	Match if TCP option *num* is set.

Table 71. TCP protocol flags

Name	Description
CWR	Congestion window reduced
ECE	ECN echo

Table 71. TCP protocol flags (continued)

Name	Description
URG	Urgent data
ACK	Acknowledge
PSH	Push data
RST	Reset (drop connection)
SYN	Synchronization
FIN	Final (close connection)

The flag combinations used in connection initiation and termination are described in Table 72.

Table 72. Typical TCP flag combinations (ECE and CWR not shown)

URG	ACK	PSH	RST	SYN	FIN	Description
				•		First step in TCP connection initiation (called the "three-way handshake").A SYN packet.
	•			•		Second step in TCP connection initiation, acknowledging the initial SYN packet and sending a reciprocal SYN back. A SYN/ACK packet.
	•					Third and final step in TCP connection initiation. Acknowledges the SYN/ACK packet. An ACK packet.
			•			Initiation of reset.
	•		•			Acknowledgement of RST.
	•				•	Acknowledgement of FIN.

Table 73. Additional TCP flag combinations considered valid by the unclean match

URG	ACK	PSH	RST	SYN	FIN
	•	•			
	•	•			•

Table 73. Additional TCP flag combinations considered valid by the
unclean match (continued)

URG	ACK	PSH	RST	SYN	FIN
	•	•	•		
•	•				
•	•				•
•	•	•			
•	•	•			•

Table 74. TCP port ranges

From	To	Description
0	1023	These "well-known" ports are in a range that most systems restrict to use by privileged processes only. The Internet Assigned Numbers Authority (IANA) controls the mapping of service names to port numbers in this range.
1024	49151	These "registered" port numbers are in a range that most systems permit ordinary user processes to use. The IANA maintains a mapping of registered service names to port numbers in this range, but does not exert control over their assignments.
49152	65535	These are "dynamic" or "private" port numbers and are not subject to IANA control or registration.

See also RFC 1700, "Assigned Numbers," for the historical (c.
1994) assignments or download the official list from *http://
www.iana.org/assignments/port-numbers* for the latest updates.

Table 75. Common TCP (and UDP) port numbers

Port	Name	UDP	TCP	Description
7	echo	•	•	Echo Protocol (RFC 862)
9	discard	•	•	Discard Protocol (RFC 863)
13	daytime	•	•	Daytime Protocol (RFC 867)
19	chargen	•	•	Character Generator Protocol (RFC 864)
20	ftp-data		•	File Transfer Protocol (Data Stream)
21	ftp		•	File Transfer Protocol (Control Stream)

Table 75. Common TCP (and UDP) port numbers (continued)

Port	Name	UDP	TCP	Description
22	ssh		•	Secure Shell
23	telnet		•	Telnet Protocol (RFC 854)
25	smtp		•	Simple Mail Transfer Protocol (SMTP)
37	time, timeserver	•	•	Time Protocol (RFC 868)
53	domain	•	•	Domain Name Service (DNS)
67	bootps	•	•	BOOTP server
68	bootpc	•	•	BOOTP client
69	tftp	•	•	Trivial File Transfer Protocol (TFTP)
80	http		•	Hypertext Transfer Protocol (HTTP)
109	pop2		•	Post Office Protocol (POP), version 2
110	pop3		•	Post Office Protocol (POP), version 3
111	sunrpc, portmapper	•	•	RPC Port Mapper (RFC 1050)
119	nntp		•	Network News Transfer Protocol (NNTP)
123	ntp	•		Network Time Protocol (NTP)
135		•	•	Microsoft: DHCP Manager, WINS replication, Exchange Administrator, RPC for Exchange
137		•	•	Microsoft: Browsing, WINS replication
138		•		Microsoft: Browsing, Directory Replication
139			•	Microsoft: File sharing (CIFS/SMB) and Print service, Directory Replication, Event Viewer, Logon Sequence, Performance Monitor
143	imap		•	Internet Mail Access Protocol (IMAP)
161	snmp	•		Simple Network Management Protocol (SNMP)
179	bgp	•	•	Border Gateway Protocol (BGP)
194	irc		•	Internet Relay Chat (IRC)
389	ldap		•	Lightweight Directory Access Protocol (LDAP)

Table 75. Common TCP (and UDP) port numbers (continued)

Port	Name	UDP	TCP	Description
443	https		•	HTTP over SSL
515	printer		•	Unix-style print spooler
563	nntps		•	NNTP over SSL
631	ipp		•	Internet Printing Protocol (IPP)
636	ldaps		•	LDAP over SSL
873	rsync		•	Rsync (see *http://rsync.samba.org*)
993	imaps		•	IMAP over SSL
995	pop3s		•	POP version 3 over SSL
1494			•	Microsoft: ICA (Citrix)
2049	nfs,nfsd	•	•	Network File System (NFS)
3389			•	Microsoft: RDP (Remote Desktop Protocol)

The Microsoft port numbers above are excerpted from Microsoft Knowledge Base Article 150543, available online at *http://support.microsoft.com/default.aspx?scid=kb;en-us;150543.*

tcpmss match

Match packets based on the TCP/IP Maximum Segment Size (MSS) header field. This match applies only to TCP SYN or SYN/ACK packets. Table 76 describes the single option to this match.

TIP

This match is available only if your kernel has been configured with CONFIG_IP_NF_MATCH_TCPMSS enabled.

Table 76. tcpmss match options

Option	Description
[!] --mss *min*[:*max*]	Match the MSS value (if only *min* is given) or inclusive MSS range (if both *min* and *max* are given).

See also:

- The --mss option to the tcp match extension
- The TCPMSS target extension.

TCPMSS target

Modify the TCP/IP Maximum Segment Size header field. Table 77 describes the options to this target. Only one of these options may be used for any given rule.

For example:

```
iptables ... -j TCPMSS --clamp-mss-to-pmtu
```

TIP

This target is available only if your kernel has been configured with CONFIG_IP_NF_TARGET_TCPMSS enabled.

Table 77. TCPMSS target options

Option	Description
--set-mss *value*	Force the MSS to *value*.
--clamp-mss-to-pmtu	Force the MSS to 40 bytes less than the Path Maximum Transmission Unit (PMTU).

See also:

- The --mss option to the tcp match extension
- The tcpmss match extension.

time match

This match extension can be used to turn packet flows on and off during specific windows of time on certain days of the week. The timestamp compared for an inbound packet is the arrival timestamp, and for an outbound packet, it is the departure timestamp. Table 78 describes the options to this match.

Table 78. time match options

Option	Description
--timestart *value*	The *value* argument is in the 24-hour format *HH:MM*.
--timestop *value*	The *value* argument is in the 24-hour format *HH:MM*.
--days *list*	The *list* argument is comma-separated list of (case-sensitive) values from this set: Sun, Mon, Tue, Wed, Thu, Fri, Sat.

tos match

Match packets based on their values for the IP TOS packet header field. Table 79 describes the single option to this match.

TIP

This match is available only if your kernel has been configured with CONFIG_IP_NF_MATCH_TOS enabled.

Table 79. tos match options

Option	Description
[!] --tos *tos*	Match if the type of service field in the IP header match the name or number *tos*. See Table 34 for a list of IP types of service.

See also:

- The FTOS target extension.
- The TOS target extension.

TOS target

Modify the IP Type of Service (TOS) packet header field value. This target extension is for use only in the mangle table. Table 80 describes the single option to this target.

Table 80. TOS target options

Option	Description
--set-tos *tos*	Set the type of service field in the IP header to match the name or number *tos*. See Table 34 for a list of IP types of service.

See also:

- The tos match extension.
- The FTOS target extension.

ttl match

Match packets based on their values for the IP Time to Live (TTL) packet header field. Table 81 describes the options to this match.

Table 81. ttl match options

Option	Description
--ttl *ttl*	Synonym for --ttl-eq.
--ttl-eq *ttl*	Match packets having a time to live equal to *ttl*. This appears in the output of the `iptables-store` command regardless of whether --ttl or --ttl-eq was used when adding a rule.
--ttl-gt *ttl*	Match packets having a time to live greater than *ttl*.
--ttl-lt *ttl*	Match packets having a time to live less than *ttl*.

For example, use this rule to have the gateway/firewall log packets with unusually high TTL:

```
iptables -A FORWARD -m ttl --ttl-gt 100 -j LOG
```

See also the TTL target extension.

TTL target

Modifies the IP TTL packet header field. This target extension is for use only in the mangle table. You can use the TTL target to mask the presence of the gateway/firewall from **traceroute** probes by incrementing the TTL for packets passing through the firewall:

```
iptables -t mangle -A OUTPUT -j TTL --ttl-inc 1
```

Table 82 describes the options to this target.

Table 82. TTL target options

Option	Description
--ttl-dec *amount*	Decrease the packet's time to live by *amount* (which must be greater than zero).
--ttl-inc *amount*	Increase the packet's time to live by *amount* (which must be greater than zero).
--ttl-set *ttl*	Overwrite the packet's time to live with *ttl*.

For example, this command sets the TTL for all outgoing packets to a very high value:

```
iptables -t mangle -A OUTPUT -j TTL --ttl-set 126
```

See also the ttl match extension.

udp match

Match extension for the User Datagram Protocol (UDP). This match extension is automatically loaded if -p udp is used. Table 83 describes the options to this match.

Table 83. udp match options

Option	Description
`--destination-port` `[!] port[:port]`	Match when the UDP destination port number is equal to *port* (if only one *port* is given) or in the inclusive range (if both *port*s are given). Ports can be specified by name (from your system's */etc/services* file) or number. See Table 75 for high-level port ranges and Table 76 for a list of common ports.
`--dport`	Synonym for `--destination-port`.
`--source-port` `[!] port[:port]`	Match when the UDP source port is equal to *port* (if only one *port* is given) or in the inclusive range (if both *port*s are given). Ports can be specified by name (from your system's */etc/services* file) or number. See Table 75 for high-level port ranges and Table 76 for a list of common ports.
`--sport`	Synonym for `--source-port`.

ULOG target

Passes packets to the **ulogd** userspace packet logging daemon (see *http://www.gnumonks.org/projects/ulogd*) over **netlink** sockets. This daemon provides more advanced logging options than the combination of the LOG target and the **syslog** facility, including the ability to log packets to a MySQL database. Table 84 describes the options to this target.

TIP

This target is available only if your kernel has been configured with CONFIG_IP_NF_TARGET_ULOG and CONFIG_IP_NF_QUEUE enabled.

Table 84. ULOG target options

Option	Description
`--ulog-cprange size`	Log *size* bytes of each packet.
`--ulog-nlgroup` `nlgroup`	Log to NETLINK group *nlgroup* (a number). This must match the configuration of a running ulogd daemon (usually in */etc/ulogd.conf*).

Table 84. ULOG target options (continued)

Option	Description
--ulog-prefix *prefix*	Prepend *prefix* to each log message.
--ulog-qthreshold *threshold*	Queue *threshold* packets before sending them to ulogd. Default is 1, maximum is 50.

See also:

- The LOG target extension, for simple logging
- The NETLINK target extension for more on netlink sockets

unclean match

Matches unusual or malformed IP, ICMP, UDP, or TCP headers. Documentation of this match is minimal (the manpage even lists it as "experimental"), but you could use it for logging unusual packets. Here are a few of the checks it performs:

IP:

- IP packet length not less than IP header length.
- Various integrity checks on any IP options.
- Various IP fragmentation checks.
- Nonzero IP protocol number.
- Unused IP bits set to zero.

ICMP:

- ICMP data at least two 32-bit words long (for required ICMP header fields).
- ICMP code appropriate for ICMP type (although some of the valid combinations in Table 32 are considered invalid by this match).
- ICMP packet length appropriate for ICMP type.

UDP:

- UDP data at least as big as the minimum-size UDP header.

- Nonzero UDP destination port.
- UDP fragmentation integrity checks.

TCP:

- TCP data at least as big as the minimum-size TCP header.
- TCP data offset and overall packet data length in accord.
- Nonzero TCP ports.
- Reserved TCP bits set to zero.
- TCP flags match one of the patterns in Table 73 or Table 74.
- Various integrity checks on any TCP options.

This match extension matches any packet that fails any of these checks.

TIP

This match is available only if your kernel has been configured with `CONFIG_IP_NF_MATCH_UNCLEAN` enabled.

There are no additional options provided by the unclean match extension.

Utility Command Reference

iptables comes with two utility commands for saving and restoring rule sets.

iptables-restore

```
iptables-restore
    [ -c | --counters ]
    [ -n | --noflush ]
```

Reads rules from standard input in the format written by iptables-save and adds those rules to the current iptables setup. Normally, tables are flushed before rules are restored into them, but you can use the -n (--noflush) option to have the new rules added to those already present. Table 85 describes the options to this command.

Table 85. iptables-restore options

Option	Description
-c	Restore the packet and byte counters for the rules.
--counters	Synonym for -c.
-n	Disable the preflushing of tables before restoration.
--noflush	Synonym for -n.

iptables-save

```
iptables-save
    [ -c | --counters ]
    [ [ -t | --table ] table ]
```

Displays rules and (optionally) byte and packet counts for all tables (the default) or for a specified table. The format is designed to be easy to parse and can be written to file for later restoration via iptables-restore. Table 86 describes the options to this command.

Table 86. iptables-save options

Option	Description
-c	Display the packet and byte counters for the rules.
--counters	Synonym for -c.
-t table	Display only the specified table.
--table	Synonym for -t.

Index

We'd like to hear your suggestions for improving our indexes. Send email to
index@oreilly.com.
